# NBA's TOP 10
# TEAMS

BY WILL GRAVES

10 9 8 7 6 5 4 3 2

SportsZone

An Imprint of Abdo Publishing
abdopublishing.com

**abdopublishing.com**

Published by Abdo Publishing, a division of ABDO, PO Box 398166, Minneapolis, Minnesota 55439. Copyright © 2019 by Abdo Consulting Group, Inc. International copyrights reserved in all countries. No part of this book may be reproduced in any form without written permission from the publisher. SportsZone™ is a trademark and logo of Abdo Publishing.

Printed in the United States of America, North Mankato, Minnesota
032018
092018

**THIS BOOK CONTAINS RECYCLED MATERIALS**

Cover Photo: Fred Jewell/AP Images
Interior Photos: Michael Conroy/Houston Chronicle/AP Images, 4–5; Mark Lennihan/AP Images, 7; Reed Saxon/AP Images, 9; Lennox McLendon/AP Images, 8; AP Images, 11; Dan Goshtigian/The Boston Globe/Getty Images, 12–13; Eric Risberg/AP Images, 15; Gene J. Puskar/AP Images, 14; Mark J. Terrill/AP Images, 16, 17; Paul Benoit/AP Images, 18; Elise Amendola/AP Images, 19; Marcio Jose Sanchez/AP Images, 20–21; AP Images, 22–23; Bob Galbraith/AP Images, 24; Michael Conroy/AP Images, 25; Fred Jewell/AP Images, 26

Editor: Bradley Cole
Series Designer: Craig Hinton

**Library of Congress Control Number: 2017962508**

**Publisher's Cataloging-in-Publication Data**

Names: Graves, Will, author.
Title:  NBA's top 10 teams / by Will Graves.
Other titles: NBA's top ten teams
Description: Minneapolis, Minnesota : Abdo Publishing, 2019. | Series: NBA's top 10 | Includes online resources and index.
Identifiers: ISBN 9781532114557 (lib.bdg.) | ISBN 9781532154386 (ebook)
Subjects: LCSH:  Sports teams--Juvenile literature. | Basketball--Records--United States--Juvenile literature. | Basketball--History--Juvenile literature. | National Basketball Association--Juvenile literature.
Classification: DDC 796.323--dc23

# TABLE OF
# CONTENTS

# INTRODUCTION

**W**hile every National Basketball Association (NBA) season is different, each one ends with a party. At the end of the NBA Finals, the buzzer sounds and a group of grown men start celebrating like a bunch of kids.

The team that won hugs in celebration. The players take turns holding the Larry O'Brien Trophy given each year to the winning team. They hold up their index fingers to tell the whole world that they are indeed No. 1. They dream about what their diamond-studded championship rings will look like.

The story behind every title team is a little different. Some teams struggle before getting hot in the playoffs. Some ride the coattails of one superstar player to glory. Some come out of nowhere and pull off an upset for the ages. This book is not about those teams.

This book is about the teams who dominated while being led by some of the greatest legends and coaches in NBA history.

# 10

Spurs players celebrate with teammates after winning the 1999 NBA Finals.

# 1998–99
# SAN ANTONIO SPURS

The NBA was in a rough spot during the 1998–99 season. The league cancelled nearly half of its 82-game schedule because of a labor dispute between owners and players. Plus, Michael Jordan had just retired after winning his sixth championship with the Chicago Bulls. The NBA needed a new team to step up. The San Antonio Spurs did just that.

The Spurs had two of the league's best big men in center David Robinson and forward Tim Duncan. They had helped San Antonio improve from 20 wins in 1996–97 to 56 in 1997–98. Going into the 1998–99 season, the Spurs believed they could be champions.

There were rumors that head coach Gregg Popovich was going to be fired if the Spurs didn't improve. In early March, the Spurs faced their archrivals, the Houston Rockets. Many thought Popovich's job was on the line. Before the opening tip, Robinson told his teammates it was time for the Spurs to start playing like they knew they could.

The pep talk worked. The Spurs beat the Rockets 99–82. It proved to be the spark they needed. San Antonio lost just two games through four playoff rounds and won the title by beating the New York Knicks.

# STEADY SUCCESS

Unlike most dynasties, the Spurs spaced out their titles. San Antonio won the championship five times between 1999 and 2014. The Spurs never won back-to-back titles and only went to the NBA Finals in consecutive years in 2013 and 2014.

In Game 5, Duncan scored 31 points, and Avery Johnson hit a jump shot to give the Spurs the lead for good. Game 5 clinched the series. A new NBA dynasty was born.

# 09

## 1986–87
## LOS ANGELES LAKERS

The Los Angeles Lakers play their home games near Hollywood. In the 1980s, the "Showtime" Lakers put on a pretty good show of their own with leading man Earvin "Magic" Johnson.

The 6-foot-9 Johnson was unlike any other player. He had the height of a forward but the speed and court vision of a guard. On a team filled with stars such as Kareem Abdul-Jabbar and James Worthy, Johnson was the ringleader.

The Lakers won five NBA titles in Johnson's first nine years. But it was a championship that the Lakers didn't win that fueled their best season. Los Angeles was the defending champion in 1986 when Houston upset them in the Western Conference finals.

Coach Pat Riley decided to finally let Johnson work his magic full-time in the 1986–87 season. The Lakers responded by winning 65 games, easily the most

in the league. Johnson won the NBA's Most Valuable Player (MVP) Award for the first time.

Johnson was even better in the playoffs. Los Angeles lost just one game over the first three rounds. A match against Larry Bird and the Boston Celtics awaited in the NBA Finals. The Lakers were up three games to two going into Game 6. Johnson saved his best for last with 19 assists in a 106–93 victory and was named the MVP of the series.

Earvin Johnson smiles after beating rival Boston Celtics in the NBA Finals.

## THREE-PEAT

The Lakers won a second straight championship in 1988, leading Riley to issue a challenge to his players. He dared the Lakers to "three-peat," meaning he challenged them to win a third straight title. However, Los Angeles fell to Detroit in the 1989 NBA Finals. The Lakers first three-peat didn't happen until the Kobe Bryant-Shaquille O'Neal Lakers won the title in 2000, 2001, and 2002.

# 08

# 1982–83
# PHILADELPHIA 76ERS

**T**he Philadelphia 76ers were an NBA powerhouse in the early 1980s. But they had two big problems. The Los Angeles Lakers and the Boston Celtics kept getting in between Philadelphia and a championship.

From 1977 to 1982, the 76ers made the NBA Finals three times, only to lose all three, including two against the Lakers. To get over the hump, the team knew it would need to get some help for star forward Julius "Dr. J" Erving. So before the 1982–83 season, the 76ers traded for Moses Malone. The 6-foot-11 center had twice won the NBA's MVP Award while playing for the Houston Rockets.

Malone turned out to be just what the Doctor and the rest of the 76ers ordered. With Malone gobbling up rebounds and patrolling the lane, the 76ers won 34 of their first 39 games and finished with the NBA's best record at 65–17.

Before the playoffs, Malone made a bold prediction. When he was asked how the 76ers would do, he responded "Fo, Fo, Fo." Malone was saying the 76ers would sweep each of their playoff opponents in four games. He nearly hit it right on the head. Philadelphia blew past the New York Knicks in the first round and dropped one game to Milwaukee in the Eastern Conference finals.

Moses Malone (2) dunks the ball against the Los Angeles Lakers.

A rematch with the Lakers awaited in the NBA Finals. Malone dominated Lakers center Kareem Abdul-Jabbar. Malone averaged 25.8 points and 18.0 rebounds per game. The 76ers won in a four-game sweep for their first title since 1967.

# 07

Bill Russell performs an acrobatic move in the 1965 NBA Finals. →

# 1964–65 BOSTON CELTICS

The Boston Celtics dominated the early days of the NBA. Even though the team's official mascot is a leprechaun, its success didn't have anything to do with luck.

The guys in the green-and-white jerseys won 11 championships in 13 years between 1957 and 1969 with a roster full of Hall of Famers. Legendary head coach Arnold "Red" Auerbach led the way.

The Celtics had some of the biggest stars in the NBA at the time, from center Bill Russell to forward John Havlicek to point guard Bob Cousy. Cousy, whose fancy passing earned him the nickname "the Houdini of the Hardwood," retired before the 1963 season. K. C. Jones took over at point guard and the Celtics kept right on humming.

They entered the 1964–65 season as defending champions but faced a serious threat from the Philadelphia 76ers. The 76ers had traded for star center Wilt Chamberlain in the middle of the season. Chamberlain and Russell were fierce rivals as the two best centers in the game. But they had very different styles. Chamberlain was a scoring machine. Russell was a defensive

wizard who loved to block shots and rebound. Those styles clashed when the teams met in the Eastern Division finals.

Boston led Game 7 110–109 in the final seconds, but the 76ers had the ball with a chance to win. That's when Havlicek saved the day. Havlicek laid off the man he was supposed to guard so the 76ers would think he was open. At the last second, he darted in to steal the pass, one of the most famous steals in NBA history.

The Celtics moved on to the NBA Finals where they beat the Los Angeles Lakers in five games. Luck had nothing to do with it.

# 06

LeBron James (23) runs down Andre Iguodala to block his shot.

## 2015–16
## CLEVELAND CAVALIERS

The Cleveland Cavaliers picked high school star LeBron James first overall in the 2003 draft. Fans hoped the teenager from nearby Akron, Ohio, could help the Cavs end decades of misery by leading the team to a championship.

James certainly did his part, establishing himself as one of the best players in the league. During his first eight seasons, however, the Cavaliers kept coming up short in the playoffs. After the 2009–10 season, James decided to try something new and signed with the Miami Heat. In Miami, he won two titles in four years. Then it was time to win one at home.

Before the 2014–15 season, James re-signed with his hometown Cavaliers. He teamed up with guard Kyrie Irving and forward Kevin Love to create the new "Big Three."

LeBron James takes in the crowd celebrating the Cavaliers' NBA title.

The Cavs fell just short of a title in 2015, losing to the Golden State Warriors in the NBA Finals. The teams met for a rematch in 2016. This time, the Warriors took a 3–1 lead in the series. It looked like the Cavaliers were going to lose once again. Then James took over. He scored 41 points in Game 5 and again in Game 6 to force Game 7.

The score was tied late when Golden State's Andre Iguodala broke loose for what looked like a wide-open layup. From seemingly out of nowhere, James came in to swat the shot away. The Cavs won 93–89. It was the team's first title and the first for a major pro team in Cleveland since 1964.

# 05

**Kobe Bryant snags a rebound at the rim against Philadelphia in the NBA Finals.**

## 2000–01
## LOS ANGELES LAKERS

**T**he Los Angeles Lakers were defending NBA champions entering the 2000–01 season. They had one of the league's best duos in center Shaquille O'Neal and guard Kobe Bryant. A repeat seemed like a lock.

The season didn't exactly go as planned. Bryant missed 14 games due to injury. O'Neal sat out eight. By the All-Star break, the Lakers had already lost 16 games. That was one more than they lost over the entire 1999–2000 season.

Lakers coach Phil Jackson had another problem. Bryant and O'Neal weren't exactly best friends. So Jackson pulled them aside. He told the two stars that the only way the Lakers could stay on top was if they became better teammates.

The pep talk worked. Bryant and O'Neal started playing more as one. The Lakers won the final eight regular-season games.

# THE O'NEAL AND BRYANT YEARS

Bryant and O'Neal led the Lakers to one more title in 2002. After losing in the 2004 NBA Finals, the team split up its two stars. O'Neal was traded to the Miami Heat, where he won a title in 2006. Bryant and Jackson stuck around to help Los Angeles earn two more titles in 2009 and 2010.

Shaquille O'Neal holds the Larry O'Brien trophy and his NBA MVP trophy.

Then they swept the Portland Trail Blazers, the Sacramento Kings, and the San Antonio Spurs in the playoffs.

Speedy guard Allen Iverson and the Philadelphia 76ers were waiting for the Lakers in the NBA Finals. Iverson poured in 48 points in Game 1 to end the Lakers' winning streak. It turned out to be just a speed bump on the way to history. The Lakers won the series in five games.

O'Neal averaged 33 points and 15.8 rebounds in the Finals. Bryant averaged 24 points, seven rebounds, and five assists. The two stars played well together. The Lakers went 15–1 in the playoffs. O'Neal called the 2000–01 Lakers the best championship team ever.

# 04

Larry Bird drives to the basket against Houston in the 1986 NBA Finals.

# 1985–86
# BOSTON CELTICS

In superstar Larry Bird, steady Kevin McHale, and hard-working Robert Parrish, the Boston Celtics of the 1980s had one of the best groups of big men in NBA history. Still, the Celtics needed help after losing to Magic Johnson and the Los Angeles Lakers in the 1985 NBA Finals.

After falling to the Lakers, Celtics president Red Auerbach went looking for the right player to put his team over the top. Los Angeles Clippers center Bill Walton was looking for a fresh start and a place to finish his career as a champion. The deal to get Walton to Boston did not come easy. The Clippers and Celtics negotiated for three months before agreeing on a trade that would send Walton to Boston for guard Cedric Maxwell.

**Bill Walton and Dennis Johnson hug to celebrate winning the 1986 NBA Finals.**

Walton made sure to hold up his end of the bargain. He won the Sixth Man of the Year Award, given each year to the top reserve player in the league. Bird was named league MVP.

Meanwhile, the Celtics made cramped Boston Garden one of the best home-court advantages in sports. Boston went 40–1 at the Garden during the regular season, the best home record in NBA history.

The Celtics hoped to get a rematch with the Lakers. Instead they faced the Houston Rockets. The Rockets had centers Ralph Sampson and Hakeem Olajuwon, known as the "Twin Towers." But the Towers and the rest of the Rockets were no match for the Celtics. Boston won the Finals in six games, its third championship in six years.

# 03

## 2016–17 GOLDEN STATE WARRIORS

One of the greatest seasons in NBA history began after an epic loss. The 2015–16 Golden State Warriors had won an NBA record 73 games during the regular season. Behind stars Steph Curry, Klay Thompson, and Draymond Green, they took a 3–1 lead in the NBA Finals against LeBron James and the Cleveland Cavaliers.

Then it all fell apart. The Warriors lost the final three games and watched as the Cavaliers celebrated on Golden State's home court. A few weeks later, help arrived. The Warriors signed forward Kevin Durant. He had been a four-time NBA scoring champion with the Oklahoma City Thunder. It took some time for all of the star players to learn how to work with each other. As they did, Golden State got better and better.

The Warriors put on a show nearly every night. Durant, Curry, and Thompson took turns torching defenses under a flurry of 3-pointers and big shots. Golden State led the NBA in scoring, averaging nearly 116 points per game. The team then breezed

**Draymond Green celebrates with the Larry O'Brien Championship Trophy.**

through the first three rounds of the playoffs, sweeping all three teams they faced.

Only the Cavaliers remained. It marked the third straight time that the two teams met with the NBA championship on the line. Golden State took a 3–1 series lead. Unlike 2016, this time the Warriors did not let Cleveland come back. Durant and Golden State buried the Cavaliers in Game 5.

The Warriors gained a measure of revenge for their 2016 collapse. Durant, for his part, gained the title he had chased for so long while playing in Oklahoma City. Durant averaged 35.2 points and 8.2 rebounds each game on his way to being named the NBA Finals MVP.

# 02

# 1971–72
# LOS ANGELES LAKERS

**E**lgin Baylor, Jerry West, and the Los Angeles Lakers of the late 1960s kept losing to the Boston Celtics. In 1968 the Lakers acquired center Wilt Chamberlain. Yet even with all that star power, they fell just short of a championship for two more years.

It looked like it might be more of the same in 1971–72, especially when Baylor retired after nine games because of knee injuries. But in their first game without Baylor, the Lakers beat the Baltimore Bullets 110–106. It served as the start of one of the most amazing streaks in sports history.

Los Angeles ripped off 33 straight wins during the longest streak by any team in major professional sports. The Lakers finished the season with a 69–13 record, the best in league history at the time.

When the New York Knicks took Game 1 in the NBA Finals, some worried that the Lakers would blow it again. Not this time. With 29-year-old all-star guard Gail Goodrich helping the "old guys," the Lakers won the next four games to claim the title.

## FROM THE COURT TO THE FRONT OFFICE

Jerry West proved to be even more valuable as a basketball executive than he was as a player. West's only title as a player came in 1972. But he helped the Lakers win four NBA Championships while working in the team's front office from 1982–2000.

# 01

## 1995–96
## CHICAGO BULLS

**M**ichael Jordan was the biggest star in sports in the early 1990s while leading the Chicago Bulls to three straight NBA titles. In the fall of 1993, the high-flying guard nicknamed "Air Jordan" decided that he needed a break. He retired at the age of 30 and spent one season playing minor league baseball.

By the spring of 1995, Jordan's itch to get back to playing hoops returned. On March 18, 1995, he told the world simply, "I'm back." Jordan rejoined the Bulls toward the end of the 1994–95 season, but he was a little rusty. The team had retired his iconic No. 23 jersey, and

**Michael Jordan slam dunks the ball against the Seattle SuperSonics.**

Jordan embraces teammate Randy Brown after winning the 1996 NBA title.

Jordan said he didn't want to take it back, so he wore No. 45. He changed his mind during the playoffs. He went back to No. 23 after an Orlando Magic player hinted that Jordan's skills had faded. The Bulls ended up losing that series to the Magic, but it helped set the stage for the greatest team of all time.

Jordan was back to his old self by the start of the 1995–96 season, and he had plenty of help. Forward Scottie Pippen was in his usual spot as Jordan's running mate. Sweet-shooting forward Toni Kukoč could make opponents pay, too.

**Coach Phil Jackson raises the Larry O'Brien Championship Trophy.**

# COACHING GREATNESS

**The most decorated person from the Bulls' championship years isn't Scottie Pippen, Michael Jordan, or Dennis Rodman. Head coach Phil Jackson won six championships with Chicago and then led the Los Angeles Lakers to five more titles. He retired from coaching in 2011 with 11 titles, the most ever by one coach in NBA history.**

Then, right before the season started, the Bulls made a trade that put them over the top. They brought in forward Dennis Rodman from the San Antonio Spurs. At 6-foot-7, he wasn't particularly tall for a forward. He wasn't very good on offense, either. But he used his long arms and his smarts to become one of the best rebounders ever.

Rodman proved to be a perfect fit with the Bulls. Chicago could beat teams at both ends of the floor. Jordan won the league scoring title by averaging 30.4 points per game. The Bulls led the league in scoring and finished third in points allowed. As the weeks rolled by, the wins piled up. In the last game before the playoffs, Jordan scored 24 points in 26 minutes in a Bulls win. Their 70–12 record was an NBA record at the time.

The first three rounds of the playoffs were a breeze. The Bulls then won the first three games against the Seattle SuperSonics in the NBA Finals. But Seattle rallied to win the next two. It was just the second time all year that Chicago lost back-to-back games. Tested for the first time in the playoffs, Jordan and his teammates pushed back. They shut down Seattle in Game 6. Jordan scored 22 points and Rodman grabbed 19 rebounds as the Bulls won 87–75 to take the series and stake their claim as the best team in NBA history.

# HONORABLE MENTIONS

**1952–53 MINNEAPOLIS LAKERS:** Led by center George Mikan, the Lakers won five titles in six years between 1949 and 1954. The team led the NBA with 48 regular season wins. This is one of the most dominant stretches by any team in history. The team moved to Los Angeles in 1960.

**1966–67 PHILADELPHIA 76ERS:** MVP center Wilt Chamberlain and guard Hal Greer led Philadelphia to a 68–13 record and the team's first title. The team also led the league in scoring and had four players average at least 18 points a game.

**1972–73 NEW YORK KNICKS:** The Knicks had been to the NBA Finals the previous year and lost to the Los Angeles Lakers. But the following season, the balanced Knicks had five players average between 15 and 18 points while knocking off the Lakers for the championship.

**1989–90 DETROIT PISTONS:** The "Motor City Bad Boys," led by Isiah Thomas, Dennis Rodman, and Bill Laimbeer, earned the nickname for their tough and physical defense. With almost 60 wins two years in a row, Detroit beat Portland to win their second straight NBA title.

**1993-94 HOUSTON ROCKETS:** With Michael Jordan away playing baseball, the Rockets and center Hakeem Olajuwon briefly took over the NBA. Houston beat the Knicks in seven games in the 1994 Finals, then swept Orlando a year later for a repeat.

**2012-13 MIAMI HEAT:** "The Big Three" of LeBron James, Chris Bosh, and Dwyane Wade won their second title in as many years. They claimed the second longest winning streak in NBA history at 27 games. And in Game 7 of the NBA Finals, LeBron finally beat Tim Duncan and the San Antonio Spurs.

**2015-16 GOLDEN STATE WARRIORS:** Steph Curry and company could have laid claim to the title of best team ever. They won an amazing 73 regular-season games, an NBA record for the best season ever. But the Warriors let a 3-1 lead in the Finals get away.

# GLOSSARY

## ASSIST
A pass that leads directly to a basket.

## BLOCK
To deflect a shot from the basket by using the hands.

## DRAFT
A system that allows teams to acquire new players into a league.

## DYNASTY
A team that has an extended period of success, usually winning multiple championships in the process.

## REBOUND
To catch the ball after a missed shot.

## STEAL
To take the ball from a player on the other team.

# MORE INFORMATION

## ONLINE RESOURCES

**Booklinks**
NONFICTION NETWORK
FREE! ONLINE NONFICTION RESOURCES

To learn more about great NBA teams, visit **abdobooklinks.com**. These links are routinely monitored and updated to provide the most current information available.

## BOOKS

Donnelly, Patrick. *The Best NBA Centers of All Time*. Minneapolis, MN: Abdo Publishing, 2015.

Graves, Will. *The Best NBA Guards of All Time*. Minneapolis, MN: Abdo Publishing, 2014.

Silverman, Drew. *The NBA Finals*. Minneapolis, MN: Abdo Publishing, 2013.

## PLACE TO VISIT

### NAISMITH MEMORIAL BASKETBALL HALL OF FAME
1000 Hall of Fame Avenue
Springfield, MA 01105
877–446–6752
**hoophall.com**

The Naismith Memorial Basketball Hall of Fame is dedicated to players in the Hall of Fame and basketball history. There are interactive exhibits, skills challenges, clinics, and shooting contests.

# INDEX

# ABOUT THE AUTHOR

Will Graves grew up in the Washington, DC, suburbs rooting every year for the Washington Bullets (now the Wizards) to win an NBA title. He's still waiting. In the meantime, Graves has spent over two decades as a sportswriter. He works for the Associated Press in Pittsburgh, Pennsylvania, where he covers the NFL, the NHL, and Major League Baseball when he's not teaching his son the art of the three-pointer.